QUICK START COACHING KIT

Mina Brown and Paula Asinof

Dedication

To all our clients, fellow coaches, other colleagues,
and especially our graduates of Coach Academy who
have challenged our thinking, stimulated our creativity,
and inspired us to write this book.

Mina and Paula

Table of Contents

Introduction to the Quick Start Coaching Kit

We know from experience and research that coaches are far better at helping people than they are at marketing and selling their services. It's difficult for coaches to explain what coaching is and how they as coaches are different from their competitors. It's intimidating for clients to buy coaching services on faith before they have experienced either coaching in general or the coach in particular.

The concept of this Coaching Kit is to give coaches an *easy* and *complete* methodology and ready-to-use tools to offer potential clients a taste of their coaching. Specifically, this Kit helps coaches market, sell and deliver their services by providing a sales script, attractive pricing guidelines, sample marketing collateral and a structured start-up coaching program. In addition, several important documents that coaches need for their businesses are included, such a client information form, coaching agreement, and coaching session prep form.

We also know that credentialing is vital in today's coaching market. As of the publication of this book, the International Coach Federation (ICF) is the globally recognized independent credentialing organization for coaches. Achieving an ICF credential requires coach specific training, coaching hours, mentor coaching, and successful completion of written and oral exams. Often training programs and mentor coaches require the recording of client sessions for evaluation and feedback purposes. This Coaching Kit includes suggestions about the process for recording client sessions, the associated confidentiality forms, and a self assessment form for the coach's personal use.

If you want to gain even more confidence in the quality of your coaching, you can purchase expert assessment and feedback of your recorded session(s) from an experienced coach. You can purchase this service ("Academy Review") at *www.mycoachingkit.com*. This is an extremely valuable investment to enhance both your coaching capabilities and your confidence.

This book is organized in two parts. Part One offers recommendations and processes for sales and pricing, marketing resources, and a structured start-up coaching program. Part Two includes several important forms specifically designed for you to use. Each form or template may be reproduced and can be customized to your business and brand.

Part One

CHAPTER 1

Sales Script and Recommended Pricing

Most coaches are deeply committed to helping others, but they are not typically trained salespeople. It is difficult for many to talk about themselves and their coaching with their contacts in a way that generates new clients. What we know is that even the most experienced sales people prepare scripts for making sales calls when they are working with a new product or service. The script can be refined based on their experience with the calls and the feedback they receive. Usually, after a few calls, the script becomes more natural and the calls flow more smoothly.

The best source for new clients is through people you know who are willing to provide referrals. To help you pitch your coaching services to these prospective clients, the sales script below is designed to get you started. As you get more experience and feedback, you will make it your own. Of course in today's busy world, you will often go into voice mail. Thus, we have provided a script for leaving a voice message that introduces yourself and gets a response.

The second most important source for new business is through networking and random in-person connections. If you are not aggressively networking, you need to be. You also need to have your business card with you at all times! And, if possible, take your calendar to set up your next appointment—most are electronic these days. When these serendipitous meetings occur, you will want to be able to introduce yourself with polish and pizzazz. For more help on developing a powerful personal introduction, check out our book *BE SHARP: Tell Me About Yourself in Powerful Introductions and Professional Bios.* You can find it on ***www.Amazon.com*** and ***www.BeSharpBook.com***.

Sales Script for In-Person Introduction

My name is _____ *[coach name].* I'm a professional coach, and I help people achieve their goals or solve their problems. In particular, my clients are _____ *[describe your niche].*

I am currently offering a special opportunity to sample my coaching at a very attractive price. In this particular program, I work with clients over the phone for five sessions.

If you or someone you know might be interested in this, I'd be delighted to talk with you. Please take my business card and let's schedule a time to talk. When would you be available next week?

Notes: _____

_____

_____

_____

_____

_____

_____

_____

_____

_____

_____

_____

_____

Sales Script for Referred Prospect

Hi, _____ *[prospect name].* My name is _____

_____ *[coach name],* and I'm calling because _____

[referral name] indicated that you might be interested in talking with me. Is this a good time for you to talk with me? . . . .

If yes, continue. If no, then schedule a time to call back.

I'm a professional coach, and I work with individuals to help them achieve their goals or solve problems that they are concerned about. May I ask you a few quick questions?

Note: this is partly sales and partly prequalifying the prospect to ensure they are a good fit for you and your coaching services.

Ask any of the following questions in any order. As soon as you get a YES, immediately go to the next section.

What would you like for me to help you with?
Listen for reply. . .

First, is there something on your mind that you would like someone objective to listen to and help you sort out?
Listen for reply. . .

Are you "stuck" in any way and need to take action that you're not sure about?
Listen for reply. . .

Are you unsure about your future or would you like to clarify your professional or personal goals?
Listen for reply. . .

Is there a decision you are struggling with and need a sounding board—someone who is not involved in the outcome.

Listen for reply. . .

If NO to all of the above:	*If YES to any of the above:*
Do you know of someone else who might be experiencing some of these challenges? *If NO, go to CLOSING STATEMENT below.*	Coaching can help. My coaching process helps you discover **your** solutions by asking questions and facilitating your thinking. I am offering a special opportunity to sample my coaching at a **very** attractive price. You don't have to make a huge financial commitment.
	We will work over the phone in half hour sessions, so it's convenient and easy to schedule. You'll be amazed at how powerful the process is and the immediate benefits you'll get.
	Does this intrigue you? Would you like to hear more?

Listen for reply. . .

If NO:	*If YES:*
Go to CLOSING STATEMENT below.	I'm offering five sessions for $ _____ *[we suggest $150 or you can set your own price].* That's only $ _____ per session *[$30 or your session price].* Would you like to give it a try?

Listen for reply. . .

If NO:	*If YES (they're seriously interested or ready to sign):*
What **would** make this work for you? Maybe just one of two sessions?	When would you like to schedule our first session?
	Let me make a note of your contact information:
	Name
	Email
	Phone and alternate phone
Negotiate to close or referral, or go to CLOSING STATEMENT below.	Street (billing) address
	How would you like to pay for this?
	If applicable, complete the **Credit Card Authorization** *form. It's included in Part Two.*
CLOSING STATEMENT:	Let me confirm our appointment _____
Thank you for your time. If you need my help in the future or if you learn of anyone who might benefit from coaching, please contact me at _____ *[phone number, email address].*	*[scheduled time/date].* Please call me at _____ *[phone number]* or I will call you. What is the best number for me to call?
	OPTION: Just so you know, if at any time after the first session, you decide that the coaching is not meeting your needs, I will refund any unused fees.
Would you be interested in being added to my mail list? *Ask for name, phone number, email address.*	I am looking forward to working with you.

Voice Mail Script

Hi, _____ *[prospect name]*. This is _____ _____ *[coach name]*, and _____ *[referral name]* recommended that I call you. I'm a professional coach, and I work with people to achieve their goals or help them solve problems.

I'm just wondering if there might be anything I could help you with. I am offering a special opportunity to sample my coaching at a very attractive price.

I would love to talk with you about how we might work together. Please call me at _____ *[phone number—say the phone number twice and SLOWLY]*.

Again, my name is _____ *[coach name]* and I'm a friend/colleague of _____ *[referral name]*, and I look forward to talking with you.

Recommended Pricing

There's general wisdom that we don't value what we don't pay for. We are suggesting a package price that we think is very affordable, and it's significantly below the typical pricing for coaching. Obviously, feel free to offer your package at ANY price that you believe is appropriate to your experience and to your prospects. We strongly recommend, however, that you don't give it away. Charging even a small fee increases the client's commitment, and it counts as paid coaching hours for certification purposes. Also tell your prospect that this is an introductory package and that subsequent sessions will not necessarily be at this same price.

> ***Recommended Package Pricing:***
> Package of five (5) half-hour phone sessions for $150

We recommend that the total fee be paid in advance. Our experience has shown that by paying in advance, the client is far more likely to complete the process. Their satisfaction with your coaching affects your reputation and your opportunity for referrals. If they drop out, your ability to support their goal attainment is diminished. There is simply more momentum and commitment and fewer barriers if they have paid for all the sessions at the beginning. In addition, your professional time is valuable. You don't want to be spending your time chasing outstanding receivables or processing multiple payments.

Note to experienced coaches: To protect your "standard" billing rate in the marketplace, you can indicate that this special coaching package is being offered in conjunction with a program that you are participating in or certification that you are pursuing—that's why the pricing is so attractive. Also feel free to adjust the pricing to a higher level if that would be more consistent with your business model in general.

CHAPTER 2

Marketing Resources

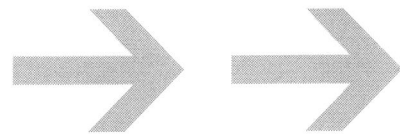

To help you talk about your program, to provide a "leave-behind", and to build credibility, we recommend that you create some marketing collateral. A simple flyer or postcard and business cards may be all you need. There are several on-line providers of professional printed materials that can be easily designed from their library of templates. One of the most widely known is VistaPrint (www.vistaprint.com) where you can order business cards, flyers, brochures, postcards, letterhead, stamps, and more at a very attractive price. Other sources include NextDayFlyers, Avery (sells paper stock and templates), or just do it yourself using the current versions of Microsoft Word (2007 and later). Word provides easy-to-use templates for a variety of marketing documents.

Here is suggested wording that you can incorporate into your flyer or other marketing documents.

Special Introductory Coaching Package

Stuck on something—need help?

Want to work on your career?

Personal issues getting you down?

Need to examine your goals—are you headed in the right direction?

Coaching can help!

Coaching is THE FRONT LINE for helping people solve problems—
personal or professional.

Coaching helps you discover your solutions.

In each coaching session, I listen.
I try to ask the right questions and challenge your thinking.

Sign up NOW to take advantage of my special introductory coaching package.
Get the benefits of professional coaching at a very attarctive price!

Five 30-minute telephone sessions
$150

We will work over the phone in half hour sessions—it's convenient and easy to schedule.
You'll be amazed at how powerful the process is and the immediate benefits you'll get.

Sign up NOW!

[Coach name] ◆ [Coach phone number] ◆ [Coach email address]
[Coach address (optional)] ◆ [Coach's Website]

CHAPTER 3

Introductory Program Structure

The goal with this kind of introductory program is to help your client focus on some specific issue, opportunity or problem that can be successfully closed within five sessions. Summarized below is a suggested structure for conducting each of these five coaching sessions. We believe this approach will produce a meaningful result for the client and valuable feedback to you on your coaching.

NOTE: All the "bold" forms and agreements indicated in the following pages are included in Part Two.

Session Structure	Suggestions

Before the First Session	• Have the client complete the
	   • **Client Information Form**
	   • **Client Agreement**
	   • **Release of Confidential Information, if applicable**
	• Collect the fee and send the invoice/receipt

In preparation for the first session, make some notes regarding:

1. Relevant thoughts about the client that you want to remember when you meet
2. Any rapport building observations, comments, or questions that are specific to this client

Notes: _____

_____

_____

_____

_____

_____

_____

Session Structure	Suggestions

Session 1:
 Building the Relationship and Goal Setting
 	
 The goal for this session is to enable the client to get more clarity about their situation and to set some parameters for the coaching engagement.
	Rapport, Co-creating the Relationship, Goal Setting
	
	 • Suggestions for opening questions:
	    • What's happening in your life?
	    • How are you doing?
	    • What going on with you?
	
	 Does the client seem to be comfortable and beginning to open up?
	
	 • What would you like to focus on in our coaching work together?
	
	 • Suggested follow up questions:
	    • How can you say it more positively (i.e. what you want rather than what you don't want)?
	    • Is this entirely within your control? (You're not dependent on someone else doing something for YOU to reach your goal.)
	    • What is stopping you from accomplishing what you want?
	    • How will you know when you get there? (What evidence will you have that you have accomplished your goal? What will it be like?)
	
	 • When you get it, how will it affect your life? Will you lose anything of value?
	
	 Invite the client to summarize their understanding of what they want to focus on. Invite them to restate the goal. Obtain agreement with the client as to any activities they will do before next session.
	
	 Schedule (or confirm) next session.

Self Assessment	• Complete your **Self Assessment Form** for this session

Notes: _____

_____

_____

_____

_____

_____

_____

Session Structure	Suggestions

Session 2: **Refining the Issue**
 	
 Goal of this session is to define the issue more clearly and gain an understanding of the "real" underlying substance.
	Rapport, Co-creating the Relationship, Progress
	
	 • Suggestions for opening questions:
	    • What's been going on since our last session?
	    • How are you?
	
	 • How did you do with your action step(s) we agreed on in our last session?
	
	 • What would you like to focus on today?
	    • Specifically what do you mean by that?
	
	 • Continue probing until you get a clear, manageable issue. Dig deeper. For example, you could ask, "If you get that, what will it mean to you?" (and possibly repeat the same question again). By the second or third iteration, you should know the real issue.
	
	 Ask Powerful, Provocative Questions
	
	 Provocative and powerful coaching often involves asking questions that challenge assumptions and offer new perspectives.
	
	 • Be curious about what the client is saying or maybe not saying. "I hear that you are usually a responsible and resourceful person, but you feel trapped right not without any options… I'm just wondering, what's different now?"
	
	 • Pursue the "truth" by asking more revealing questions. "What do *you* think the real truth is here?"
	
	 • Provoke contemplation and insight by asking doubting questions. "Are you sure about that? I have a sense that there's something more."
	
	 Designing Actions, Planning and Goal Setting
	
	 • What is one thing you can do right now to move forward? Are you willing to do it? How are you going to hold yourself accountable?
	
	 Invite the client to summarize their understanding of the "real issue".
	
	 Invite them to restate their action steps.
	
	 Schedule (or confirm) next session.

Self Assessment	• Complete your **Self Assessment Form** for this session

Notes:

Session Structure	Suggestions
Session 3: *Digging Deeper* *Goal of this session is to trigger a shift. It's the "cross over" session where the client takes ownership of the issue and begins to design a "new normal"—the way they want their future to be.*	**Rapport, Co-creating the Relationship, Managing Progress** • What's been going on since our last session? • How did you do with your action step(s) we agreed on in our last session? • How are you feeling about it? **Ask Powerful, Provocative Questions** • Suggest something more: More possibilities. More concepts. • Suggest something different: Offer distinctions, different frameworks, or invite them to make a change. • Suggest something less: Possible absence of something, eliminate the source of the problem, or decline participation in something. **Designing Actions, Planning and Goal Setting** • What is the next most important thing you can do to move forward? • What resources do you need? (tangible, financial, or emotional) • Which ones do you already have? Which ones do you need to get? • How are you going to get them? • If you need an emotional resource (e.g. confidence), is there a time when you had that? Can you apply that experience here? • What could get in your way? • What are you committed to doing right now? • When specifically will you do it? *Invite the client to summarize their understanding of insights and action steps from this session.* *Schedule (or confirm) next session.*
Self Assessment	• Complete your **Self Assessment Form** for this session

Notes: _____

_____

_____

_____

Session Structure	Suggestions
Session 4: **Problem Solving and Recording, if applicable** *Goal of this session is to continue the progress from Session 3 in issue clarification and action planning.* *If you are planning to produce a recorded session for certification purposes, program requirments, or professional coaching feedback, this is the best session to use.*	**Communicating Effectively, Managing Progress** *If you are intending to record a coaching session, this is the best one. Right at the beginning of the session, turn on the recording, and confirm with the client that they are aware of the recording and have agreed.* • How are you? What's been going on since our last session? • How did you do with your action step(s) we agreed on in our last session? **Ask Powerful, Provocative Questions** *Refer back to Session 2 or Session 3 for additional suggestions.* • _____ • _____ • _____ **Action Planning, Wrap Up** • What is the next [most important, most obvious, best] thing you can do to move forward now? *Invite the client to summarize their understanding of insights and action steps from this session.* *Schedule (or confirm) next session.*
Self Assessment	• Complete your **Self Assessment Form** for this session. If the session was recorded, conduct the self assessment by listening to the recording.

Notes: _____

_____

_____

_____

_____

_____

Session Structure	Suggestions
Session 5: *Action Planning and Closure*	**Managing Progress, Action Planning** • What's been going on since our last session? • How did you do with your action step(s) we agreed on in our last session? **Action Planning, Wrap Up** • What's different now than when we started? • What progress have you made in addressing your issue? • How do you know you've made progress? What evidence do you have? • When we finish today what are you going to do differently? • How are you going to maintain it? • What might keep you from achieving your goal? What are the possible barriers? • What is the benefit, if any, to you for avoiding a change? • What will you do about it? *Invite the client to summarize their understanding of their overall progress and commitments.* • How can I help? *Offer additional coaching, if appropriate. Schedule the next appointment.* *Explain the* **Client Feedback Form** *and request their assistance when they receive it. (See next page.)* *Ask for referrals.*
Self Assessment	• Complete your **Self Assessment Form** for this session

Notes: _____

_____

_____

_____

_____

_____

Session Structure	Suggestions
After the Program is concluded	• Send the **Client Feedback Form** to the client. • If applicable, schedule and complete your Academy Review or other professional review of the recorded session. • Send a follow-up "thank you note" and remind them of your services. Be creative… include a suggestion about exactly how your coaching services might be useful to help them accomplish a specific goal or an especially challenging part of their action plan.

Notes: _____

_____

_____

_____

_____

_____

_____

_____

_____

_____

_____

_____

_____

_____

_____

_____

_____

_____

CHAPTER 4

Recording Client Sessions

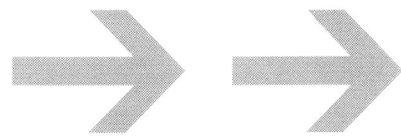

Recording a client session is an excellent way to improve your coaching. First, you have the opportunity to listen to your own performance and evaluate how well you did. You can use the **Self Assessment Form** to guide your evaluation. Second, you can give your recording to another professional coach for their objective feedback. As mentioned previously, you can purchase an expert assessment of your recorded session(s), an "Academy Review", at ***www.mycoachingkit.com***. Finally, some coaching certifications require submission of a recorded client session. In order to create a quality recorded session, "practice makes perfect".

Preparation for Recording

The application for certain coaching credentials (e.g. ICF) requires the submission of a recorded coaching session. Ideally, the recording should be approximately 30 minutes and should demonstrate your skills in as many of the coaching competencies as possible. You probably cannot use a tape made during your coach training. It is imperative to check with the certifying organization for the most current requirements.

In order to cultivate self confidence and master the recording process, begin making trial recordings now and continue until you have a satisfactory recording.

General Guidelines and Tips

1. Make sure you get the appropriate signed release forms from your client for each recording. If you are submitting a recording to the ICF for certification purposes, you must use a specific ICF form. For convenience we have included a copy in Part Two of this Kit. You will need to send it to the ICF along with your recording. Also if you are considering having this recording evaluated by an Academy Reviewer, you need to have a ***separate release form*** signed by your client. This form is also included in Part Two.

2. Ensure that the environment is conducive to coaching and a good recording. In particular, turn off call waiting on your phone—check with your provider for

instructions. Also, you should be in a quiet space without background noises (e.g. pets, children, appliances). Consider using a headset to reduce these noises.

3. State at the beginning of the recording: your name, the date of the session, and the first name of the client. Have the client confirm that they have agreed to the recording, that they understand the confidential nature of coaching, and that they understand that the recording may be submitted to a professional reviewer. Here's an example:

    "Ed, as you know, I am recording our confidential session, and this recording might be heard by a professional reviewer. You already signed a release form. Would you please confirm that you are aware we are recoding this session and have agreed to do so? [Wait for affirmative response.] For the record, this is Sally Brown, and I am recording my coaching session with Ed on February 10, 2010."

4. Be sure to demonstrate coaching competencies as well as possible. Plus, stick with coaching—stay out of consulting, mentoring, teaching, advising, etc. If you happen to use something other than coaching, be sure to ask permission of your client to use the other mode.

5. Listen more and talk less. The client should be talking more than the coach.

6. Relax and enjoy engaging with your client. Show your enthusiasm for coaching.

7. Listen to your recordings and use Part Two of the **Self Assessment Form** to evaluate your skills.

8. If you are sending your recording to a reviewer or certifier, select a recording that has a wide variety of skills demonstrated. Also, check to be sure the voice quality is clear and loud enough to be heard easily and that there are no background noises.

Recording Services

1. There are several free conference lines available on-line that offer free recording capabilities. It's very easy to use, and the quality is excellent. Your client will need to call into the conference line which is usually a long-distance phone call.

2. Use a search engine to find one of these service providers. Check to ensure that the calls can be recorded for free. The on-line provider will give you a dedicated "on-demand" dial-in number, an access code, and a moderator "PIN" that don't usually expire.

3. You will need your PIN for starting and stopping the recording and for downloading your recordings later. Also, you MUST download your recording as soon as it's available (the site will usually send you an email with the access link). Otherwise, your next recording might overwrite the prior recording, losing it forever.

4. These recordings are usually in an MP3 format, which is acceptable for the ICF.

5. You might also want to consider making your calls through the Internet using "Skype" technology: ***www.Skype.com***. A Skype account is free, and it comes with recording capabilities. We recommend using a computer headset for better sound quality on Skype.

Part Two

Templates & Forms

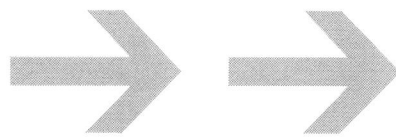

Client Information

Name: _____

Title: _____

Company: _____

Preferred email address: _____

Mailing Address: _____

_____

Business phone: _____ Mobile phone: _____

Home phone: _____ Fax: _____

Birthday (month, day): _____ Time zone: _____

What is your past experience with coaching? _____

_____

_____

_____

_____

Other information relevant to our coaching: _____

_____

_____

_____

_____

_____

This information is obtained solely for purposes of our coaching engagement. No information is shared with any third parties for marketing or other purposes without your express permission.

Coaching Agreement

Client Information

Name: _____

Telephone: _____

Email: _____

1. **Client Fully Responsible:** As a client, I understand and agree that I am fully responsible for my physical, mental, and emotional well-being during my coaching sessions, including my choices, decisions, and actions. I am aware that I can choose to discontinue coaching at any time.

2. **Coaching Boundaries:** I understand coaching does not involve the diagnosis or treatment of mental disorders nor is it a substitute for professional advice by legal, medical, financial, business, spiritual, or other qualified professionals.

3. **Mental Health:** I promise that if I am currently under the care of a mental health professional, I have consulted (or will consult) with the provider regarding my working with a coach.

4. **Confidentiality:** I understand that information will be held as confidential unless I state otherwise, in writing, *except as required by law*. I understand that coaches are not covered by "privilege" in a court of law. I understand that certain topics may be *anonymously and hypothetically* shared with others for training or consultation.

5. **ICF Coaching Log:** I agree that my name, contact information, and documentation of total coaching hours may be provided to the International Coach Federation (ICF) for purposes of coach certification review. This information is maintained in confidence by ICF.

6. **Fees and Payments:** Unless otherwise arranged, I understand that fees are payable in advance. I understand that I may be charged for "no shows" or appointments cancelled with less than 24 hours notice. I understand that my paid session starts at the scheduled appointment time. Any dispute regarding services is limited to fees paid. I understand that from time to time, my coach may refer people to other coaches or other professionals and also may obtain referrals from others, some of which involve arrangements by which referral fees are paid.

I have read and agree to the above.

Client Signature: _____   Date _____

Release of Confidential Information

Purpose: The purpose of this release is to facilitate the ICF credentialing application of

_____
(Name of credential applicant)

I, _____ , authorize _____
         (Name of client)   (Name of credential applicant)

to record and release the following audio-recording to the International Coach Federation (ICF).

Information to be released: Audio-recording of my coaching session on _____
                                                                                          (Date)

Permission to release to:

International Coach Federation
Credentialing Coordinator
2365 Harrodsburg Rd.
Suite A325
Lexington, KY 40504
USA

I understand that the audio recording of my coaching session will be reviewed only by ICF Application Review members, who will use it for the sole purpose of assessing the quality and methods of my coach. I understand that the information will be kept confidential and will not be shared with any other party.

This release form has been read/reviewed with me and I understand its content.

Client Signature: _____   Date _____

Client Signature: _____   Date _____

Release of Confidential Information
for an Academy Review

The purpose of this release is to facilitate my coach's learning and coaching development.

I, _____ , authorize _____
  (Name of client)   (Name of coach)

to record the following coaching session and to release the audio-recording to the Academy Reviewers. I understand that the information will be kept confidential.

Information to be released: Audio-recording of my coaching session on _____
                                                                                                              (Date)

Permission to release to:

Academy Review
Attention: Mina Brown
6107 Jereme Trail
Dallas, TX 75252
USA
www.mycoachingkit.com

I have read and reviewed this release, understand its content, and agree to the recording and release.

Client Signature: _____   Date _____

Credit Card Authorization

Client Name	
Date of Authorization	
Charge Amount	$
Credit Card Type	American Express ☐ MasterCard ☐ Visa ☐ Discover ☐
Credit Card Number	
Credit Card Expiration Date	**Card Security Code** *Required*
Credit Card Name Exactly as on the Card	
Company Name	
Billing Address	
City, State, Zip	
Phone number	
FOR RECEIPT: Fax number or Email address	
Signature (if in person)	

NOTE: Credit card information is NOT maintained by this company/coach. For your security, this information is destroyed after all charges have been processed.

Terms, Special Instructions, Comments:

_____

_____

_____

_____

Coaching Session Prep Sheet

I have found that preparation ahead of time will help you to get the most out of our sessions and the coaching experience. The simple acts of debriefing your activities between sessions, taking credit for your successes, analyzing your roadblocks, and articulating your needs for assistance can be <u>invaluable</u>. However, it is completely OPTIONAL. If you choose to use this simple tool, please email it to me as soon as possible before our appointment. Preparation will expedite our work and help me <u>help you</u> in the most efficient and effective way possible!

1. What have I accomplished since our last session? What am I most proud of?

2. What have I learned about myself or others? How will that inform future actions?

3. What are the most important challenges I am facing now?

4. What are the particular opportunities available to me right now?

5. I want to use the session to:

6. Anything else?

Client Coaching Log

Date	Client	Hours	Billable	Prepaid	Pro Bono	Comments

Self Assessment Form

Client Name	

The ICF competencies are the industry accepted professional standards for quality coaching. More information about these competencies can be found at the International Coach Federation website (***http://www.coachfederation.org/***). This form has been designed to provide specific evaluation against these standards.

Use this form after each session with each client to evaluate your coaching. Consider how well you stayed present, listened deeply to your client, asked provocative questions, helped your client make a "shift", and design actions. Then use the second part of the form to specifically evaluate how well you applied each of the ICF competencies. You will find as you coach that certain competencies apply more directly to some sessions than to others.

In Part One, record your general notes about each coaching session. In Part Two, we recommend using a rating system to note all the competencies you demonstrated in each session and at what level. The goal is NOT to get a "perfect" score. The value of the chart is to give you a quick perspective of how well your coaching aligns with these professional standards over the course of your engagement.

Part One: Session Self Assessment

Session Date	What I learned	What I can do better	Primary Competencies Demonstrated
Session 1 Date			
Session 2 Date			
Session 3 Date			
Session 4 Date			

Session Date	What I learned	What I can do better	Primary Competencies Demonstrated
Session 5 Date			
Overall Evaluation			

Part Two: Competency Self Assessment

Rating system:

Excellent: 3 points ♦ Good: 2 points ♦ Needs Improvement: 1 point ♦ Didn't cover: 0 points

ICF Competency	Session 1	Session 2	Session 3	Session 4	Session 5
A. Setting the Foundation					
1. Meeting ethical guidelines and professional standards					
2. Establishing the coaching agreement					
B. Co-creating the Relationship					
3. Establishing trust and intimacy with the client					
4. Coaching presence					
C. Communicating Effectively					
5. Active listening					
6. Powerful questioning					
7. Direct communication					
D. Facilitating Learning and Results					
8. Creating awareness					
9. Designing actions					
10. Planning and goal setting					
11. Managing progress and accountability					
Total Points (maximum 33)					

Client Feedback

Your feedback and input is extremely important to me to improve my coaching abilities. Thank you so much for completing this evaluation and returning it to me at your earliest convenience.

Name	
Date Completed	

Please rate the following with respect to your coaching experience with me. Comments explaining your rating would also be appreciated.	Excellent	Good	Fair	Poor
Overall coaching experience	❏	❏	❏	❏
Comments:				
Clarity in setting objectives for coaching sessions	❏	❏	❏	❏
Comments:				
Progress in meeting coaching goals	❏	❏	❏	❏
Comments:				
Ease of access for scheduling and communication	❏	❏	❏	❏
Comments:				
Listening, support and encouragement	❏	❏	❏	❏
Comments:				
Additional comments:				

	5 Definitely	4 Probably	3 Maybe	2 Unlikely	1 Never
On a scale of 1-5, how likely are you to recommend me to a colleague or friend?	❏	❏	❏	❏	❏

Who would you recommend that I contact who could benefit from my coaching?

Name: _____ Phone: _____ Email: _____

Name: _____ Phone: _____ Email: _____

Thank You!

About the Authors

Mina Brown

President and Founder, Positive Coaching Group
www.PositiveCoach.com

President and Co-founder, TurnKey Coaching Solutions LLC
www.TurnKeyCoachingSolutions.com

President and Co-founder, Coach Academy Texas LLC
www.CoachAcademy.biz

Mina Brown is an experienced executive coach, business consultant, and career consultant. Through her three companies, she offers one-on-one coaching, large-scale coaching programs, and professional coach training. Earlier, she was both a CFO and Operations executive of a large public company. She is the National Career Transitions Coach for *6FigureJobs.com*. Mina is a Certified NLP Coach, a member of ICF, CoachVille, and a founding member of IAC. She is a CPA and holds an MBA from Vanderbilt University's Owen School.

Paula Asinof

Principal and Founder, Yellow Brick Path
www.YellowBrickPath.com
blog.YellowBrickPath.com

Paula Asinof, a career management coach and resume expert, is a catalyst for accelerating careers. She helps successful executives and professionals move up or move on. Her background includes executive search, executive coaching, career services, and senior corporate positions in Information Technology and Finance. She holds the prestigious designation of Credentialed Career Manager (CCM). She is also a Certified NLP Coach, Certified NLP Practitioner, and ICF member. She holds an MBA from the Wharton School.

Check out another popular book by the authors.. . .

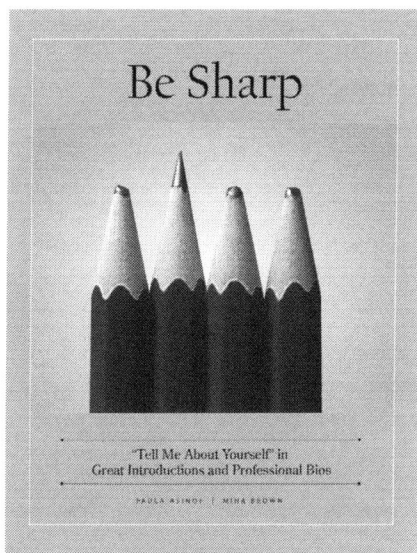

Be Sharp:
"Tell Me About Yourself" in Great Introductions and Professional Bios

This book will help you deliver a personal introduction with professional polish and pizzazz.
You will have confidence to introduce yourself in any situation, anytime, anywhere.
In addition, when you incorporate this methodology into your coaching, your clients
will gain a fresh perspective by talking with you in rich detail and in positive terms.
You will also have learned a great deal about your client.

Available on-line at *www.Amazon.com* or *www.BeSharpBook.com*.

Made in the USA
Charleston, SC
28 September 2015